WATER: RICHES OR RUIN

by Helen Bauer

CALIFORNIA MISSION DAYS
CALIFORNIA RANCHO DAYS
CALIFORNIA GOLD DAYS
WATER: RICHES OR RUIN

Riches (Karl Obert, A.P.S.A.)
or
Ruin (California Division of Forestry)

WATER

RICHES OR RUIN

Helen Bauer

DOUBLEDAY & COMPANY, INC.

Garden City, New York

1959

Dedication

To my brave father and mother, who took their
three young children, Helen, Ralph, and Dorothy,
to live on the Mojave Desert during the construc-
tion of the Los Angeles Aqueduct. Though many
years have passed since then, memories remain
vivid . . . memories of coiled rattlesnakes, the wild
howling of the coyotes, the grace of leaping deer
over greasewood, the hillsides aflame with golden
poppies, and the endless humming of the cement
mill grinding limestone into cement for miles of
tunnels that would bring water to Los Angeles.

CONTENTS

Acknowledgments

The author wishes to express her genuine appreciation for the contribution of other authors who have written on the subject of soil and water conservation and for the assistance given in the compilation and collection of all material that has made this book possible.

There have been many agencies that have furnished the abundant pictorial materials, such as The U.S. Forest Service (S.F.); U.S. Dept. of Agriculture (Washington, D.C.), Soil Conservation Service (Berkeley), U.S. Bureau of Reclamation (Sacramento), Division of Forestry (San Francisco) and the California State Resources Bureau (Sacramento). In each office the personnel was co-operatively interested and generously responsive in furnishing maps and pictorial material and in providing needed information.

Photographs were secured from and credit is hereby given to Hubert A. Lowman, my good friend who has had photographs in all of my books; Karl Obert (photographs furnished by Pearl Chase, Calif., Conservation Council, Santa Barbara), and George Borst. In addition, the John Deere Co. (Moline, Ill.) provided the photograph of contour planting in the form of a flag; the L.A. Times of reseeding by heliocopter, and the Tennessee Valley Authority several photographs.

The San Francisco Water Department and the Los Angeles City Dept. of Water and Power were helpful in giving information and maps concerning aqueduct systems.

Generous credit is given to the able editorial staff of the publisher for their patience and understanding as well as their valuable editorial assistance.

One must also acknowledge the help, understanding, and co-operation of family members. In particular, I give credit to my husband, Roy M. Bauer, for his patience, encouragement, and help in the map drawing and to my son, Dr. Sherwin Carlquist, my valued critic, who gave this book its provocative title, and to my daughter, Roberta Logerman, for her constant interest and affection.

Preface

Man has always thought of water as his FIRST need. There is just so much water. If there is not enough for one man's needs he will fight for it. Men have fought for water in the past. They are still fighting to get more. It is important that we have enough water tomorrow as well as today. As the nation grows, so grows the need for more water. In the future there will be uses for water that we have never dreamed about. Where will we get it? This is something that concerns all of us. Plans have to be made to save and use water wisely.

We want the story of water to have a happy ending. We do not want a land of waste or ruin. We want OUR land to be a place where there is plenty for all now and in the days to come.

(Soil Conservation Service—U.S.D.A.) *

For a strong America we must use our natural resources wisely.
Let's start by learning the conservation pledge.

CONSERVATION PLEDGE

"I give my pledge as an American to save and faithfully to
defend from waste the natural resources of my country—its soil
and minerals, its forests, waters, and wildlife."

* Wording in poster is pledge of a group, not that of one person as given below.

15

WHAT CAN I DO?

What can I do in conservation
To aid my community, state, and nation?
I can use courtesy, thought, and care,
In field or forest everywhere.
Take what I need, but never waste;
Curb my desire for frantic haste.
In handling forest, range, or field
Plan skillfully for future yield.
Observe the laws for fish and game
And help my neighbors do the same.
So live that in a future year
None will regret that I passed here.

by WOODBRIDGE METCALF
from *Conservation: Concern for Tomorrow,*
Bulletin of the California State Department of Education,
Volume XXIII, No. 1, February, 1954.

1. America—a present land of plenty

THIS IS OUR land—the United States of America. Wherever you are, wherever you live—as a proud American you are a part of this great and beautiful country. This is a rich land with huge, busy cities and many towns. There are farmlands with broad fields of waving grain, green crops, and fruits of all kinds. Cattle graze on rolling hillsides. It is a land of flowing rivers, wandering streams, mountains with thick forests, lakes with wooded banks. Land-loving and water-loving animals have their homes in forests and streams. Rich minerals such as gold and silver are stored deep in the earth. The wealth that we have comes from the land and from water.

Much of our land has been damaged already. Water and wind have ruined over three billions of tons of our best cropland. This much would fill a train of cars going around the world eighteen times! One fourth of the farmland that once existed in this country has been destroyed by poor farming. Farmers have not always been careful about preventing

Nature's gifts are our resources (California Division of Forestry)

water and wind erosion in their fields. Fields have been plowed up and down slopes rather than across so that rainfall and irrigation water ran down and carried valuable topsoil away. Several million California acres, for example, have lost over half of their topsoil through erosion. Farmers in some areas have planted the same kind of crops year after year until many minerals needed for growing crops have been used up. Some of these minerals could be replaced by fertilizers. Sometimes too many cattle, especially sheep, have been allowed to graze on land until the land became bare. Men have not worried about cutting down too many trees. Many places do not have enough water. In other places there are terrible floods. Minerals have been wasted. People in earlier times thought, as many do today, "There will always be enough." Now we know that this is not true. We have been wasting nature's gifts to us.

Nature's gifts are our resources. People have not always thought how much they depend on nature. In the United States we have always used all the things given by nature—the forests, grasses, animals, and the soil and water that give

18

Saving the land is like flying a flag full-mast! (Deere & Company)

them life. We have called these our natural resources. For all these years we have had all of the natural resources we have needed. We have taken from nature but we have forgotten to give back. Some of the resources, such as soil, water, and trees, can be renewed. Even so, it takes a long time to do it. Oil and minerals, once used, are resources that cannot be renewed.

Ask yourself the question, "Will this be a land of plenty when I am grown?" And, "How about the years after that?" This plenty is ours to share NOW, but will we always have it? There is still time to decide how the story of America will end. Will it be a country of waste—or one of plenty? Unless we STOP, THINK, and PLAN, we could be a poor country.

To keep what we have, we must use wisely and without waste what we have. This does not mean part of our resources —but ALL. And not alone, but TOGETHER, nature and people. We live in a land where everyone wants to do his part and is allowed to do so. YOU live at just the right time to have an important part in America's future.

2. What does conservation mean?

CONSERVATION is a plan by which nature's gifts —our resources—may be used wisely. To conserve is to use what we need, to take care of these resources for the most people for the longest time. So the plan works in the present but also keeps in mind the future.

A man may think of his money in the same way. He may save it and use little of it, or he may spend it, having just enough for the present. Another way is for him to use what he needs and still leave some for later use. We should think of our resources, nature's gifts, in much the same way. Use them, don't waste them, and leave enough for those who come after us.

To know what and how to conserve, we must know more about nature's gifts. We need to know the ways of earth, water, and weather on hill and mountain, field and forest.

20

Wildlife has a part in the conservation story (Karl Obert, A.P.S.A.)

The conservationist knows about swift rivers, the rich soil, the green forests, the wonders of wild life. He knows that each one of them has a part in the plan of living. They are all part of the CONSERVATION STORY. You will want to know more about them too. You will see how each depends upon the other. Together they help to make America what it is today.

As we grow as a country, so our use of resources grows. We need more wood for paper, rayon, plastics, lumber. We

21

must find out better ways to take care of our forests and plant life. We have to find out how to use water more wisely. We cannot grow as a nation if our resources, the riches of nature, are not conserved.

Water brings life to the land (California Water Resources Bureau)

3. How nature works

FOR hundreds of years animals, soil, and plants, forest and water have worked together to keep nature in balance.

Wherever we live we all have a place called home. Animals and plants need places to live, too. So the forest is not just land covered with trees. Trees shelter many kinds of animals which make their homes in and among them. What a pleasant home for birds living high in leafy branches! They flit from place to place, carrying seeds and eating harmful insects. Other birds find safe homes on many lakes. The frisky squirrel gathers and buries acorns. If he does not dig them up, oak trees will grow. Bees carry yellow pollen from flower to flower. Beavers build dams. With their sharp teeth they cut down trees and bushes. Then they build a wall of branches across small streams. On top they slap mud with their flat tails. Because of this little hard-working engineer his dams hold water that might run down too fast.

Animals that live in the forest depend on the kind of soil

23

Beavers build dams that hold back water (U.S. Forest Service)

that is there. Without good soil there would be no fine forests. Plants and animals play an important part in making good soil. Animals make holes in the earth and keep the soil loose. Plant roots grow and help to break up rocks into smaller pieces. For millions of years nature has been grinding up rocks to make soil. Snow, ice, and wind have changed rocks into tiny particles.

Plants and trees drop their leaves—yellow, brown, and red. Pine trees drop their slender dry needles. They float

24

down to rest under the trees. There they act as a sponge to soak up water that would otherwise run off. Other things mix with this litter of leaves—dried twigs, fallen branches, old

The forest is not just land covered with trees (U.S. Forest Service)

25

logs. Sooner or later animals die and their bones become part of the earth. The bones add minerals to the soil. After a time rains and snow cause the mixture to rot or decay. The result is a rich, soft black soil we call humus. This humus is crumbly, soaks up water, and is rich in minerals so important for plant life.

Foresters think of the soil, plants, and animals as all depending on each other. Without thinking or planning they take from and give to each other. Each form of life plays its part.

Each form of life—plant and animal—depends on water. Plants and animals drink from the ground. Water sinks into the earth and passes up through the tree. When it reaches the leaves and is warmed by the sun, it goes off into the air as vapor. We call this **evaporation.** The vapors rise and come together to form clouds. When the clouds have more water vapor than can be held, water falls to earth in the form of rain or snow. Once more the cycle or circle starts over again. Nature takes care of its own resources in a wonderful way. It is only MAN who changes nature's work.

4. *How man changed nature's work*

WHEN the white men came to America, they found a land much different from that of today. They found the Indians, the animal and plant life all living there. Nature's wealth was all around them. What a strange and beautiful world, these settlers thought! In the early days Columbus wrote, "Always the land was of the same beauty. Fields were green . . . the fruits red . . . the perfume of flowers . . . the singing of birds—very sweet."

Almost all the Eastern part of the country and the mountain areas had great forests. A springy carpet of dead leaves lay under the old trees. Animals and insects, birds, fish, and plants lived in the forests. There was plenty of food, shelter, and living space for all of them.

Between the forested lands of the East and West were the Great Plains. Here was a different kind of land. There were few trees, but the wide rolling plains were covered with

27

thick grass. Here, just as in the forests, the animals and plants lived and worked together.

At that time not much was known of the West. We know, however, that Indians, plant, and animal life lived together peacefully there, too.

America might have gone on this way, but the white man began to make changes. These men wanted to have large farms, build homes, have herds of cattle. They needed houses, furniture, ships. It seemed to these people that trees were in their way, like weeds. Get them out of the way! They needed lots of land but they took more than they needed. So—down came the trees!

What happened when so many trees were cut down? The earth was left without its blanket or "ground cover." Water rushed down the slopes. Soil began to muddy rivers and small streams. Stream bottoms filled with good topsoil called silt. Streams had less room to flow and often flowed over their banks. Floods brought down more and more silt. This was the start of trouble that has kept up through the years.

Buffalo that lived on the grassy plains were killed or driven from their homes. Grasslands became plowed fields. Thousands of plants and animals died. Their places to live were destroyed. Grazing cattle ate the grass too short. Their hoofs cut the grass until it died. It is in such places that dust storms later blew away many tons of topsoil.

As towns and cities grew up, there was need for more and more lumber. Sometimes lumbermen cut down too many trees. Without trees water ran away without doing any good.

Settlers kept moving farther and farther west. There was always new land to be found and used. What if trees were cut down? What if good soil did wash into rivers? There always seemed to be plenty of good soil left.

These early Americans did not think of the future—only the NOW. We shall see what happened later because they did these things. Not only was nature harmed, but the result was to harm people, too. Gradually more and more people saw that there was no new land close at hand. They had to make the best use of what they had. They saw that they had to get along with nature. This was the beginning of conservation in America. Soil and water conservation is the modern way of working with nature.

They plowed too much land (U.S.D.A.)

5. *Our good earth—the soil*

SOIL means life. Man is a land animal. He lives on the land and gets what he needs from the land. You may say, "How can soil mean life to me?" First of all—to live, all of us must have food, clothing, and shelter. Did you ever ask yourself, "Where do these things come from? Where did the Corn Flakes I had for breakfast come from? And the bacon and eggs?" Some food comes to you in the form of fruits and vegetables which grow in the soil. The soil grows plants which feed cattle and chickens, which in turn feed you. If it were not for the soil, you would have no food.

Where did the cloth for your warm coat or your dresses come from? Cotton and linen come from plants. Wool, fur, and leather come from animals. Some rayon is made from wood. If your house is made of wood, thank the soil for growing trees. Much of the furniture in your home can be traced to soil too. The very paper in this book came from the trees that grew in the good earth.

What is soil? It is not the dirt you sometimes get on

30

your hands and face. It is not rocks. You can think of soil as a mixture of many things. Soil has water and it has fifteen kinds of minerals that make plants grow.

Have you ever looked at a handful of soil? If you have, you would have seen that some is black, some brown, some gray, red, or yellow. Some soils are sandy, some like powder, and others are heavy clay. All soil has vegetable, animal, and minerals in it.

Soil is not the same everywhere in our country. Unlike the carpet of humus on the forest floor, some land may have very rocky soil. In some places the soil may just cover the rocks. In still other places the soil may be several feet deep. This soil is not the same all the way through. If you dug a hole, you would find that the first few inches are different from the soil below it. The rich layer on top is called topsoil. It is the

Erosion survey of the United States (Soil Conservation Service—U.S.D.A.)

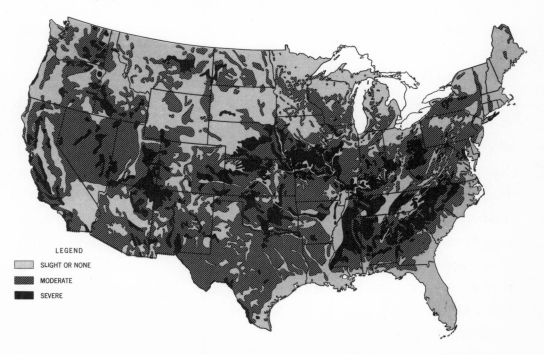

LEGEND

SLIGHT OR NONE

MODERATE

SEVERE

31

Working with nature to save the soil (Soil Conservation Service—U.S.D.A.)

richest part of the soil. Topsoil makes good crops. The vegetables we eat need topsoil. So do the grasses of the pasture and the ranges where cattle feed. The soil below is subsoil. Subsoil makes poor crops but it is important as a place to store water.

Can nature keep on making good topsoil for us? Yes, but it takes a long time. Scientists have found that it takes hundreds of years to make just one inch of topsoil! One good heavy rain could wash that much away! Once gone, it cannot be brought back again. Look in your back yard or at a hillside after the next rainstorm. Do you see fine soil or silt that has been carried down a slope? In all such places part of the good topsoil has been washed away. Every year a half million or more acres are lost in just this way. We call it EROSION, or the eating away of soil. This soil erosion is one of the biggest problems on farms today.

32

Wouldn't you think that Americans would treasure this precious soil? Many Americans have; many more have not. George Washington, our first president, studied ways of keeping water from carrying away topsoil. Thomas Jefferson, another president, was a wise and careful farmer. Still another of our presidents, Theodore Roosevelt, once said, "When the soil is gone, man will go."

When a bank is robbed, every newspaper tells the story. But our soil upon which people depend is robbed of about a half million dollars' worth of soil every year! Very few pay any attention to this kind of news. But the soil is a real bank. Deposited in the soil is the wealth of our country. If we are to keep on living as well as we have, our topsoil must be saved.

Who is to blame when good fields become barren? Early settlers wasted because there was plenty. But there isn't plenty any more. It would seem that we today are doing little better than the early-day Americans. We must think of these things before it is too late. What will happen in a few years? Imagine a country without good soil to grow food. Saving the soil is not the worry of the farmer alone. He would be the last one to starve. It is important to ALL of us, wherever we live, in whatever city or town. The soil affects each of us in all parts of the country.

Nor is soil conservation the work of grownups only. It is the work of every boy and girl who loves his country. Boy Scouts, Girl Scouts, 4-H Clubs, Future Farmers, and schools are all helping. Sometimes planting even one tree gives aid to water, grasses, wild life, or man. Seeding a slope does the same. Whenever you see muddy water flowing, you know that there is work to be done to save soil from washing away. Our American way of life depends on our "good earth."

6. *All life must have water*

WE COULD have all the gold in the world, but without soil and water it would do us no good. Soil is important, as we have learned, but we must have water. To be useful, water and soil must work together. Not one blade of grass would grow in any soil if it did not have some water. With water, animals and plants live; without it they die. Is it any wonder that we say that water is our most important resource?

You turned on the faucet in your home this morning. There was water necessary for your health and to keep you clean. This did not seem so wonderful to you. But it would have seemed wonderful to the people of long ago.

Some of the people of early times caught rain water in jars or bowls. Some had to dip their water from lakes, rivers, or springs. To get it to their homes, they had to carry it in jars or bags made of skins. So villages and towns grew up by rivers and around lakes.

34

In the little pueblo (village) of Los Angeles, California, the people went to the river for water. Water had to be brought to the fields to grow crops. A large ditch (*zanja*) was built. "But," said the women, "we still have to carry water to our homes in jars!" So a Mother Ditch (Madre Zanja) was brought to the pueblo. Those farther away from the ditch had to have water brought by water carriers. These people knew that they could never live in their new pueblo if there were not enough water for all their needs.

So man has always thought of water as his FIRST need. There is just so much water on the earth. If there is not enough for one man's needs, he will fight for it. Men have fought for it in the West ever since cattlemen battled over the first water holes for their cattle. Men are still fighting to get more.

This may be hard to believe, for there seems to be plenty of water everywhere—lakes, rivers, oceans. This is true. Look at a world map or a globe. You will see that there is more water than land. It would seem that there should be enough for all. The trouble is that water is not always where

Water being brought to places where it is needed (U.S. Bureau of Reclamation)

it is most needed. And not all of it is usable, such as the salt water in the great oceans.

In some places, as in parts of California, there has not been enough water in the dry times of the year. The same is true in many other parts of the country. There is not enough rainfall in some places; in others it runs away to the ocean without doing any good. Water is wasted in many ways.

How much do you think you use every day? About thirty-five to one hundred gallons are used by each person each day. Many people use a great deal more. Before the days of plumbing, washing machines, and heating systems a family used about eight gallons a day. Now, suppose that there were no water for an hour, for a day, or even a week. It is possible to live without food for a month. We could not go without water longer than three or four days.

Your clothes came from a mill where water and electric power were used. Last night you slept in a house made of lumber from a forest. Without water we would have none of these things.

36

Water is important to both the plants and animals of the earth. Think of how much water is needed for all living plants! Trees need even more water than people. On a hot day the roots of a big tree may drink up more than one thousand gallons of water! It takes four thousand gallons of water to grow just one bushel (thirty-two quarts) of wheat. Again, think of how much water is needed in factories to make goods for all the people of our country.

Today water has become more and more important to man. He needs it in his home whether in the city or in the country. He needs it for irrigation of crops, as waterways for travel, and for his recreation. It is important that we have water tomorrow as well as today. As the nation grows, so grows the need for more water. We have more and more people in the United States. Will there be enough water for all in the years to come? This is something that worries people. Plans have to be made to save and use water wisely. We cannot begin too early to think about the importance of water to all of us.

Lake behind Shasta Dam used for boating and fishing (U.S. Bureau of Reclamation)

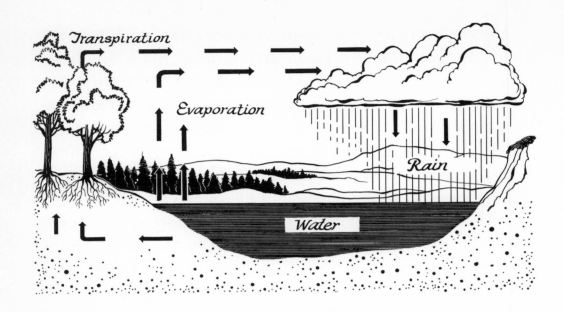

7. *Water makes a magic circle*

SINCE water is so important to all living things, we should know more about it. The story of water is an exciting and wonderful story.

Where does water come from in the first place? We know that it comes from the sky as rain. How did it get there? It is interesting to see how nature takes care of this.

The story of water begins with the sun itself. Hang wet clothes on the line. Out comes the bright sun and clothes are dried. After a rainstorm streets and sidewalks are wet. Soon they are dry again. What happens? There is only one way water can get into the air. We say that it evaporates. Water in the air is called water vapor.

Water vapor is all around you, in your home and outdoors. There is always some water vapor in the air. Water is always changing into water vapor. You can see water when it is a liquid. You can see it frozen as snow or ice. But you cannot see water as vapor. You cannot feel water vapor, either, because it is not wet. Water vapor is a gas.

38

Hold a lid over the spout of a steaming teakettle. Or blow your breath on a mirror. Do you see the tiny drops of water that form? The hot steam or warm breath hit something cold, as air. Then water vapor formed into little drops of water like a mist.

Try something else. Suppose that it is a hot day. You have a glass of iced lemonade. Look closely and you will see drops of water on the outside of the glass. It looks as if the water had come right through the glass! No, the water came out of the air around the glass. As long as the air was warm, the water vapor stayed in the air. But when the air was cooled by the cold glass, water vapor formed into little drops on the glass. When we SEE the water, we say that it has CONDENSED. Water vapor has turned into drops of water.

Now put a glass jar over a small growing plant. Look later and you will see tiny drops of water on the inside of the jar. What happened there? The plants gave off water vapor into the air while they were growing. When the water vapor from the plants on the inside of the jar hit the cold jar, drops of water were formed. Where there are many trees, as in parks or forest, there is water vapor in the air. Haven't you noticed how much cooler it is where there are many trees? In deserts, where the air is very dry there are fewer plants.

Water evaporates from the surfaces of rivers, lakes, and oceans. It evaporates from everything that is wet. It moves from place to place and is never lost. When the vapor rises from bodies of water it mixes with the warm air. Warm air rises toward the sky. The warm air gets cooled. Now the vapor is changed into tiny drops of water. Look into the sky and see the dark clouds. These dark clouds are masses of tiny, tiny drops of water. As more water vapor turns into drops of water, the clouds become darker. After a time the drops of water get so heavy they cannot stay up in the air. They begin to fall out

39

of the air. It is raining! Water has returned to the earth again. Next time you see a dark cloud in the sky you may say, "That is a lot of tiny drops of water. The water disappeared from way down here. Now it is way up there!" If it is freezing cold in the cloud or in the air around it, the water vapor changes into small crystals of snow. Snowflakes fall from the sky and we say that it is snowing. Sleet is partly frozen rain or a mixture of rain and snow. Hailstones are small pellets or balls of ice which are frozen raindrops.

The way water leaves the earth and comes back again is called the WATER CYCLE, which means "water circle." From ocean, to sky, to earth, and the circle starts all over again. Water keeps moving in a wonderful way!

Much of the rain falls back into the ocean. Some of it swells the rivers, lakes, and small streams. Some wets the soil for thirsty trees and plants. Still more sinks into the earth. Sometimes the water that sinks into the earth bursts out again as a spring. The water from the spring may go tumbling down the side of a mountain to form a small river or rivulet. Little rivers join big rivers until they run at last to the tossing ocean. Rivers pour into the ocean day and night. The ocean spreads over three fourths of the earth. From the top of the ocean the water is evaporated into the air again.

Some rains are so heavy they are called cloudbursts. Of course a cloud does not really burst. A cloudburst happens when the air below is so strong it pushes upward and rain cannot fall. If no rain falls for a long time, a large amount of water is massed together. When the rain finally comes, it falls very fast. Records of many cloudbursts can be found. Usually they cause a great deal of damage. Rich soil is carried away, too.

If water always comes back, why must we be careful not to waste water? Water does return, but not always when or

40

Little rivers flow on to join big rivers (U.S. Bureau of Reclamation)

where it is needed. If no rain falls for a long time, water must be saved. We shall find out later how this is done. Sometimes water is in clouds, but we cannot get it down. Scientists have worked on that, too. Streams may get dry. Reservoirs or storage places may get almost or entirely empty. Some parts of the country are drier than others. People have trouble getting enough water.

8. *Where water goes that falls on the earth*

OVER a billion million gallons of water fall as rain in the United States each year. This means that there is a rainfall of about thirty inches. That much is enough to cover the whole country with two and a half feet of water. But every place in the United States does not get that much. Some places get as much as one hundred inches, some no more than five inches. Some years there are places that get no rain at all. We cannot choose where water will fall. Man must make the best use of WHAT water falls and WHERE it falls.

About one half of the rainfall goes off in water vapor, drawn up by the sun. About one sixth runs off into streams and to the ocean. The rest goes into the ground.

Now we can see why we learned about soil first. Soil and water are related and work together. More often than not, when you conserve soil, you conserve water, too. Suppose that rain falls on poor, hard soil. If the land slopes, most of the water runs off. This is what we do not want to happen. If the rain falls on soil covered with plant life, it sinks into the ground. Water that goes into the ground is called "ground water." Down deep in the earth are layers of rock. Down goes the water into these layers.

After a while the soil above the layers gets full of water. The top of this water is called the WATER TABLE. If a lot of rain falls, the water table is high. Suppose that there is a dry season or perhaps the water has run off. The water table is low. The water line, or table, goes lower and lower. Now, if a well is dry, it must be dug deeper into the earth. The water table may be so low no water at all is found.

Water in the ground is very important. We draw upon it for many things. Men dig wells and draw out water for farms and cities. Plant roots reach down and get their water from it. The water table stores water like a tank under the ground. It feeds springs and streams during dry times of the year. Water must be stored in the water table to get it out later. More cannot be taken out than goes in.

To be of use later, water must soak into the ground. Trees and other well-rooted plants help to hold the soil in place. What happens when rain falls in the forest? Water

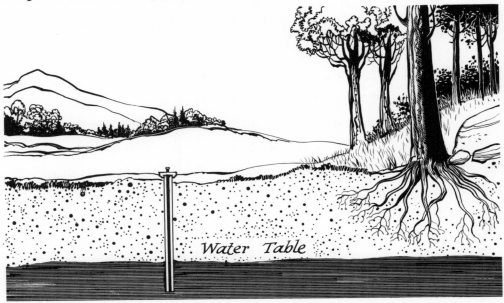

Water Table

If a slope is bare, water rushes down, carrying soil with it (U.S. Bureau of Reclamation)

drips from the leaves. Rain falls down upon a thick blotter-like carpet of leaves and twigs. If the soil is as hard as subsoil, raindrops hit as tiny hammers on the bare soil. This loosens the fine part of the soil called silt. Water then carries the good topsoil away. This is just what should NOT happen.

Suppose that rain falls in the mountains. If there are lots of trees, bushes, and grass on the slopes, water will be "blotted up" or run down slowly. If the slope is bare, water will rush down, carrying soil with it. A watershed is a wooded slope where water or melting snow can be stored.

44

You can see how very important it is to have plant life growing on watersheds. In this way water is held back and kept from running away too fast. Later this water will feed into springs and streams. Floods are caused when watersheds are bare. Water, mud, and rocks roar and roll down mountainsides. Everything in the path is either damaged or destroyed.

In the West, the mountain lands give cities most of their water. Melting snow sends water to lands below long after the rainy season is over. We shall see later what happens when fires destroy trees and other plant life that grow on watersheds.

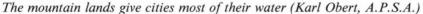

The mountain lands give cities most of their water (Karl Obert, A.P.S.A.)

9. Water—a soil thief

WE USUALLY think of water as our friend. It supplies so many of our needs, and nothing living could do without it. Did you ever stop to think that water can be an enemy also? Water can be a "soil thief." Remember that when water falls on the soil three things can happen. Some water evaporates and goes into the air. When the land is level and not too hard, rain sinks into the ground. Some of the water runs over the surface of the earth and on to streams or rivers. If the last happens, it has the power to destroy.

It is the nature of water to flow. When it finds a place to run downhill swiftly, it can be an enemy. At first there may be just a trickle. Then more water follows . . . faster, faster, faster . . . more, more. If nothing is done to stop it, water will carry a whole field downstream and to the ocean. Soil and water are mixed together. And that is what water can do and very often does, eat away the soil. Then we have an enemy—erosion.

When a raindrop hits bare soil, it kicks up a tiny splash of dirt. Soon a small hole is made in the earth. After the next rain, look around your house. Do you see holes made by

The Grand Canyon where the Colorado River has cut deep into the land (Hubert A. Lowman)

dripping water from the roof? This is SPLASH EROSION. Just a few drops don't do much damage. Think of millions of drops splashing down onto the earth. There is an old saying, "Water can wear away even a stone." This is true, and bare earth wears away much faster than rock!

If water keeps running in the same place for a long time, a gully or ditch is made. Each time it rains, the gully is cut deeper into the soil. This kind of eating away of the soil is called GULLY EROSION. A gully once started is likely to grow deeper and deeper until something stops it. This has happened often in places where brush or trees have been cut or burned. Since the land was left bare, the water rushed down, taking with it soil and sand. This is one way that streams and rivers steal good earth from the land and carry it to the sea.

Many years ago, water dripping from a barn in Georgia started a gully which became famous. Nothing was done to stop it and the gully kept on growing. First, it swallowed up the barn, then the whole farm. After that a schoolhouse, several houses, a church, and other farms were washed away. And all this because of the dripping of water from a barn. Patrick Henry, one of our early Americans, once said, "He is the greatest patriot who stops up the most gullies." Now you can see why he said it.

FINGER EROSION cuts small paths like the fingers of an outstretched hand. If these "fingers" are not taken care of, they will grow larger with each rainfall. They may even form gullies.

Then there is SHEET EROSION. This cannot be seen so easily as gully erosion. It skims like a sheet over the top of a small hillside or sloping field. Water carries away a thin sheet of topsoil. Usually this is the richest part of the soil. Slowly, slowly this rich soil is carried down from stream to stream— and to the ocean. Only the poorest soil is left.

48

Little gullies can become big gullies (Soil Conservation Service—U.S.D.A.)

Wasted water—damaged land and crop (Soil Conservation Service—U.S.D.A.)

Land on the march (U.S.D.A.)

Men have found that fields planted in crops lose more soil than grasslands. You probably know the reason. Planted crops have loose, bare earth between the rows. Grass grows close together and has matted roots. The roots, of course, hold back water long enough to let it soak into the ground instead of running off.

The greatest loss of soil ever measured in the United States took place on a steep slope in California. The land had been planted in long rows of beans. Between each row the soil was bare. Three inches of rain fell and carried away five hundred tons of soil from every acre!

It has been found that erosion spreads from farm to farm. Topsoil from one farm can be washed down onto

51

another farm. The farmer may say to himself, "I am lucky! My neighbor's loss of soil is my gain!" He is wrong. His neighbor's soil was sandy and rocky and covered his best topsoil. His land then held less water and his own soil washed down onto another neighbor's land. This shows how neighbors have to work together to save soil.

All over America water is carrying away the soil. It is the good topsoil that is needed. You can see how important it is to keep water from stealing away soil. Good soil does no one any good at the bottom of a river! This is land wealth that is being lost. It is like money that drops through a hole in a pocket. It is time that we thought about sewing up the hole in Uncle Sam's pocket!

Rushing water not only carries down good soil; it causes terrible floods. Newspapers often tell us of floods in different parts of the United States. Almost every year heavy rains or melting snows cause quiet streams to become wild rivers. Streams rise, swift and dirty. Fields and towns are flooded, homes destroyed, bridges washed out. People lose their lives.

One of the worst floods in recent times happened in the West. It was Christmas time. Millions of people were making ready for a happy holiday. Then the heavy rains came. Rivers flowed over their banks. People in northern California, southern Oregon, and western Nevada began to worry. Before the floods were over, there were many deaths and millions of dollars' worth of damage. Every year something like this happens somewhere in the United States.

The loss of the water itself is as bad as losing the good soil and having floods. The water runs away instead of sinking into the ground and later being put to good use. This water is needed as much as, if not more than, the topsoil. Americans are beginning to know more about soil and runaway waters and are doing something about it!

52

10. Making running waters slow down

MANY WAYS are used to stop land from being "eaten away" or eroded. Of course the best way is to have croplands that do not slope too much. In this way water does not have a chance to run fast downhill.

Have you ever seen a farmer plowing in a field? How proud he is when he plows a straight row! But suppose that all or part of his land is hilly. He has to find a way to make rows that are not straight but will make water "walk" instead of running.

Sloping land planted up and down lets water run downhill. Large amounts of soil can be carried down. So, instead of the farmer plowing up and down, rows are made across the hill. Water is held in the rows long enough for it to sink into the earth. This kind of planting is called CONTOUR PLANTING. Rows follow the curve or the contour of the hillside.

Another way to slow down water is by TERRACE PLANTING. Terracing is used on steeper slopes. Terraces are like steps on the side of a hill, each a little higher than the other. Broad, shallow strips of land are cut across the slope. Crops

Making a plan for the land—contouring (Soil Conservation Service—U.S.D.A.)

A terracing program (Soil Conservation Service—U.S.D.A.)

Strip cropping to save soil and water (U.S.D.A.)

are planted in these terraces, or steps. The terraces hold back both water and soil when heavy rains come. Hillsides are kept from washing down.

STRIP PLANTING is still another way to hold soil in place. Broad strips are plowed across a slope. Grass or low-growing crops with a thick sod (as clover) are planted between the strips. On the level strips the farmer plants crops such as corn or wheat. Again, water is held in the ground instead of running away.

What happens when the farmer does these things? Topsoil is left in place so that his crops are better. His land is worth more. Floods are stopped before they start. His soil does not wash down on his neighbor's land. Streams do not fill up with silt or fine dirt. Neither do the storage lakes behind dams. Water is used but not wasted. It stays where it is needed for crops.

Farmers are learning how to build up the land by planting different kinds of crops in succeeding years. They know that chemicals are needed in good soil. Scientists tell us that there are at least fourteen chemical elements necessary for good plant growth. These elements for plants come from the air, water, and the soil. If plants do not get these elements (such as nitrogen, calcium, potash, phosphorus), the farmer has to do something about it. He has to add chemicals and fertilizer to the soil. Crops such as peas, clover, alfalfa, when plowed under, add nitrogen to the soil. Other crops, cotton, corn, wheat, take certain chemicals out of the soil. So the farmer "rotates" his crops and does not plant the same crops in the same place year after year.

Soil Conservation Districts have been formed in many areas of the United States. This is important not only to the farmer but to all of us, for they work to protect our land and water resources. There are nearly three thousand such conservation districts in the United States, Hawaii, and Alaska. Farmers in a district form groups that decide WHAT they want to do, WHEN they want to do it, and WHOM they want to help them. No federal or state government agency can order them to form these groups. But the government experts are willing to help and always do when they are needed. This is American teamwork, with people and government joining together to work out plans in their own way for the good of all.

Suppose Tom Brown were worried about his farm. For several years he had not earned as much money from it as he thought that he should. He looked over his fields. He thought, "If I don't do something soon, I won't have any crops in a few years."

So he joined the Soil Conservation District. Someone was sent from the Soil Conservation Service to help Tom. He took samples of the soil. He made a map of the farm. It showed the slopes, the wooded parts, the places that had the best soil. Together they planned what was best to do. They made a "land use" map that showed what was best for every part of the land. Then Tom went to work. Some parts were left for pasture. These he left in grass. He plowed around the curves of the hills. He had planted corn year after year in the same place. He decided that he would plant wheat instead.

After a few years he had nature working with him on his farm. The soil was better, so water was held where it was needed. His crops were much better. His neighbors watched Tom and did the same thing. It paid off for all of them. When farmers have good crops, city people are helped too. They must buy what is grown on farms.

Gullies can be stopped by the building of small dams of earth or stones, brush or logs. Vines and bushes can be planted along the sides—anything that will keep water back. If the cause is removed, erosion can be stopped.

A Soil Conservation Service expert testing the soil and planning use to be made of the land (Soil Conservation Service—U.S.D.A.)

Today much of our cover of trees and grass that was once here is gone. What we have wasted we cannot get back. But we can take care of what we have. If we are to remain a great nation, this must be DONE.

A soil conservation plan to improve farm crops

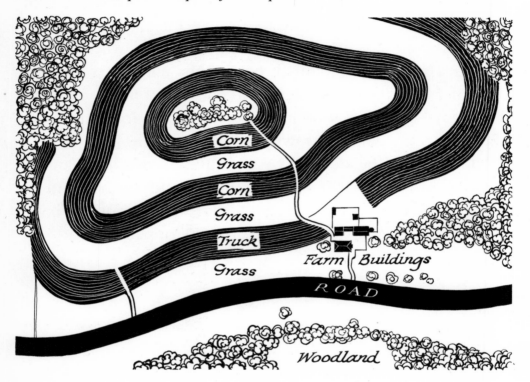

58

11. *Kinds of erosion; how they can be stopped*

WIND is a "soil thief" also. Have you ever thought that wind could carry away soil? Where light soil is dry and bare it is fine like powder. Along comes a strong wind. It whips at the soil and sends it flying. Watch a whirlwind zigzag across a dry field. See the huge clouds of dust? When this happens many times in the same place there is WIND EROSION. Much of the soil carried away is good soil.

In 1934, in just one dust storm, several millions of tons of soil were blown away! Some of it blew from the middle part of the United States clear to the Atlantic Ocean! Dust piled up against homes, barns, and fences like snowdrifts. Dust rose in the air like smoke from a forest fire. Even the sun could not be seen on a bright day. This has happened in parts of our country several times. Such places are called "dust bowls," and nothing green can be seen any more. Thousands of people have left their homes and farms in the "dust bowl" and have gone to live somewhere else.

Good soil blown away by the wind (Soil Conservation Service—U.S.D.A.)

One way that man caused wind erosion was by plowing the land too much. Now this kind of erosion has to be stopped. It can be helped by planting grass that holds the soil. Just as a captain anchors his boat to keep it from drifting, so the soil must be anchored down. Plants are the anchors that keep soil from blowing away. This takes a long time to do. Trained men are trying to help farmers plan how to use wind-eroded land. There is still a great deal to be done. We are still losing one and a half million acres each year from such erosion.

Another way to keep the soil from blowing away is to plant trees and bushes and by cross wind strip-planting. Windbreaks of trees help to keep wind from blowing across wide-open spaces. Large numbers of trees have been planted in "dust bowl" areas.

Once the cattle ranges were covered with thick grass. But men put too many cattle and sheep on the ranges. The short grass was eaten down to the roots. Then the many hoofs cut up the topsoil and grass roots. Animals kept tramping around looking for food. They packed the soil down until nothing could grow in it. When the grass was gone, wind and water took the soil away.

At the end of the grazing season there should be three to six inches of grass stubble left. This stubble gives protection against wind and water erosion. Animals should not be allowed to graze on land until the new (spring) grass has had a chance to grow. If ranges are well managed, cattle are better fed and so bring a better price in the market.

Once this grazing land was covered with thick grass (U.S. Bureau of Reclamation)

Eroded slope before *planting (Tennessee Valley Authority)*

The United States passed a law that kept the land from being grazed too much. Only so many cattle or sheep could be put on a range at one time. They had to be moved from place to place. Just as trees make a forest, grass makes the range.

Too many trees have been cut down in the forests. Men know now that they must not cut down so many trees, especially on slopes. Only the largest trees should be cut for lumber. Smaller ones can help to keep the soil in place, and they are the forests of the future.

Eroded slope after *planting (Tennessee Valley Authority)*

Too many roads have been built without thought of erosion. Often the sides of a new road are left bare. When soil is left bare, runoff water has a chance to go to work. Erosion is the result. Bare slopes should be planted with bushes or a ground cover of vines or small plants.

We know that we must USE our land. But it must be used in a wise way. We must keep valuable soil from being carried away by either wind or water. The earth gives us a great deal. We in turn owe the earth our care.

63

12. Fire—cause of floods

FIRE is one of our worst enemies. Fire ruins green ground covers. Once trees, shrubs, and grasses are gone, erosion begins. Bare, hard earth cannot soak up water. Water cannot do anything but gnaw its way downward. Flood waters are wild waters that destroy. Such water, which could be used, is wasted.

Forest fires leave ugly, bare hillsides. How are such fires started? Some say that they are started by lightning. Only a few fires are started that way. Usually it is man who starts forest fires. He does not plan it that way. It is because he has been careless. Perhaps all he did was to throw away a lighted match. It fell into dry grass. Crackle . . . hiss . . . and soon a whole hillside was on fire.

Perhaps it was caused by a campfire left with glowing coals. The fire only seemed to be out. A wind sprang up. Smoke boiled upward. Red tongues of flame licked their way up slopes. Soon a terrible fire was racing through a beautiful

Red tongues of fire ran up the mountain slope (U.S. Forest Service)

After trees are destroyed, water will rush down the watershed (California Division of Forestry)

forest. Animals fled from their homes. Great trees fell in the path of the flames. Perhaps it was days before the fire was put out. Men risked their lives. Thousands of acres of trees and green plants were burned over. What a waste! All this because of a burning match!

Think of the years it took to grow such trees! Young people would be men and women before these trees were that tall again! How black, barren, and ugly were the hillsides that remained! Perhaps worst of all, what would happen when it rained? Water would rush down the bare slopes.

We have learned that watersheds are slopes that hold rain water and snow. This is nature's storage place or reservoir. It is the best and cheapest way of storing water. The soil on a watershed must be able to absorb water like a sponge. Roots, rotted leaves, and twigs help to keep the water in the soil. Trees hold back the heavy packs of snow.

If there is a fire and trees and shrubs are burned, the watershed cannot hold water. Water cannot be held back for

This watershed can no longer hold water (U.S. Forest Service)

later use. Sometimes watersheds can he repaired. This is done by planting seeds on the slopes. The United States Forest Service plants the seeds by helicopter. Usually mustard seed is dropped on black hillsides. Mustard grows quickly and forms clumps to hold the soil. Mustard plants last about four years. During this time the brush has a chance to grow again. Sometimes the soil is so scorched that seeds may not grow in it for several years, maybe never. In some places, where too many trees have been burned, young trees have to be planted. Many of our state governments, the federal government, and private companies grow trees from seed.

Imagine how you would feel if you lived in or below a burned-over area. Not only is the fire frightening but there is nothing so terrifying as water rushing out of control. Such floods caused by fires have happened many times. One of the worst such floods happened in Southern California. There were two canyons, one green, the other burned over by fire. Heavy rains came. There was no watershed to hold back

Mustard seed is dropped on black hillsides (Los Angeles Times)   67

Forest rangers sit in high towers watching for forest fires (California Division of Forestry)

Speed in putting out the fire is important (U.S. Forest Service)

water in one canyon. The racing water struck against houses in the way. Some were washed down the slope. Others were piled high with muddy water and rocks. Down the water raced to towns below! Hundreds of other houses were damaged. Some people knew about the flood in time, others did not. Many never lived to tell what happened that night! The same amount of rain fell in the other canyon. But little damage was done where the green watershed held back the flood water.

Forest rangers are our friends. They try to see forest fires when they are small. They sit high in their towers in the mountains . . . watching, watching. If they see smoke, they telephone for fire fighters. Fire fighters try to be there before the fire spreads. Speed in putting out the fire is important. The forest rangers do their share but they need help from all of us.

Everyone should obey fire rules posted in forests and other places. You can be careful yourself. And you can remind others to be careful too. You can be a "private-eye detective" and watch to see that they do obey rules. "Smokey the Bear" posters are used all over the United States to remind people of the dangers of forest fires.

Some rules we are all asked to remember are:

Break matches before throwing them away. Then you will know that they are out.

  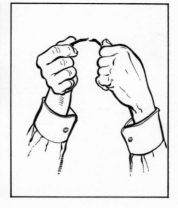

Make a safe campfire and clear a space around it.

Never leave a campfire until the coals are "dead out."

Use lots of water.

Smokey the Bear is a fellow we would like to help. We are told that fire burned out nine million acres of forests last year. We can help by remembering that ONLY *YOU* CAN PREVENT FOREST FIRES. Which would you rather do—prevent a fire or fight it?

"Take no chances with fires when you are about,
They are so easy to start, so hard to put out!"

Today automobiles and paved highways take thousands of people into the beautiful green national forests. Who would go if these same places were black and barren? Forest fires should NEVER happen! Let's keep America green!

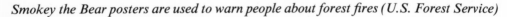

Smokey the Bear posters are used to warn people about forest fires (U.S. Forest Service)

13. Water and dams

WE KNOW that floods are caused by rushing water. This water can be saved for good uses. Millions of dollars have been spent to build great concrete dams. Some are as high as tall buildings. These concrete dams are built in canyons so as to hold back water. Many are built across rivers so that the water flow is stopped. Water cannot get over the wall, so it backs up. Storage reservoirs or lakes behind dams are made in this way. Gates in the dam may be opened wide, halfway, or just a little, as water is needed.

In parts of the Western United States there are many places where there are no streams or rivers. Rain does not fall during the summer, the hottest and driest time. Man has learned to build dams and canals so that water can be brought from many miles away to where it is needed.

Life-giving water for homes, farms, and industries comes from reservoirs behind dams. Los Angeles, for example, gets most of its water by canals and pipes from the reservoir be-

Building Shasta Dam (U.S. Bureau of Reclamation)

hind Hoover Dam many miles away. The Hoover Dam across the Colorado River (between Arizona and Nevada) is the tallest (726 feet high) dam ever built in the United States. The lake behind it (Lake Mead) is the largest lake (119 miles long) ever made by man.

The second-highest and largest dam in the United States is Shasta Dam (*Northern California*). Water from Shasta Lake flows down the Sacramento River in California. Still farther down water goes into canals and is used on farms, in towns and cities.

The Grand Coulee Dam on the Columbia River (between Oregon and Washington) irrigates more than a million acres. Once this was a very dry land. With this water the land can now grow fine crops. It has cost millions of dollars to bring water to these dry lands, but the food raised because of this water is worth even more.

Did you ever see high waterfalls tumbling down over rocks? Did it seem to have great power as it tumbled down?

Shasta Dam completed (U.S. Bureau of Reclamation)

There is power in falling water, and engineers have learned how to use it (U.S. Bureau of Reclamation)

There IS lots of power in falling water, and engineers have learned how to use it. Water is held behind dams. Finally it is allowed to spill through gates in the dam. It works the same as a waterfall and has great power. From this falling water man has learned how to make power that turns wheels. These wheels run engines that make electricity. This kind of power is called HYDROELECTRIC, or WATER (hydro) POWER. The electricity can be sent over wires to farms and cities many miles away. When you press a button in your home and light comes on, think of water that may have made electricity for you.

What happens if water flowing into the storage basin (reservoir) or lake is muddy? Mud is heavy and it settles to the bottom. After a while the lake fills up with mud or silt.

Water from dams to irrigate dry lands (U.S. Bureau of Reclamation)

Electricity is sent over wires to farms and cities many miles away (Tennessee Valley Authority)

There is less and less space left for water. This is still another reason why it is important to keep soil from being carried away by water. When a lake behind a dam fills with silt, why not shovel it out? This is sometimes done by scooping the silt out with heavy machines. It has been found that it costs as much or more to clean out silt than it does to build a new dam. Besides, when silt and sand are cleaned out, it must be piled somewhere else. The next rainstorm may wash it back into streams.

Lakes behind dams are beauty spots. Thousands of people enjoy boating and fishing in such lakes. Nearly all Americans like to leave crowded cities. They like the out-of-doors. It is an important part of our present American life.

75

14. *Getting water to farms*

THE FIRST thing a farmer has to think about when he gets a farm is water. Perhaps the farm is near a stream. The horses and cows could use such water. But often river water is not good for drinking. It could be that people farther upstream threw their waste into the water. Or perhaps a mill threw its waste and used water into it. The farmer has to be sure that there is good clean water for his family's use.

He must be certain that there is water for use on his farm during all of the year. When there is no rainfall, he must have water for irrigating, or watering, his crops. Irrigation is often the difference between making money or losing everything the farmer has. The good farmer with plenty of water can raise good crops. Without it he cannot grow good crops.

Anyone who has watered his lawn or garden knows something about irrigation. It is man's way of doing a job nature decided NOT to do—giving water to thirsty soil. Today in the United States we are using twenty-five trillion gallons of water to irrigate twenty-five million acres.

76

Water has to be brought to dry lands (U.S. Bureau of Reclamation)

If the farmer does not have water from a nearby stream or from rainfall, he might have to dig a well. You remember about the water table. Deep in the rock layers water is stored. Pumps are needed to pull the water up to the top of the ground. The more water that is taken out, the lower the water table goes. The well might even go dry. In Arizona many farmers depend on irrigation for their farms. Almost all of it comes from underground. In some places the water table has dropped over fifty feet in a few years. Some land has already gone back to desert because there was not enough water.

The best way for the farmer to get water is to make use of that stored behind dams. Sometimes this water has to be brought many miles by canals and ditches. Water can be brought to the place where it is needed when it is needed.

With this water the land can grow fine crops (U.S. Bureau of Reclamation)

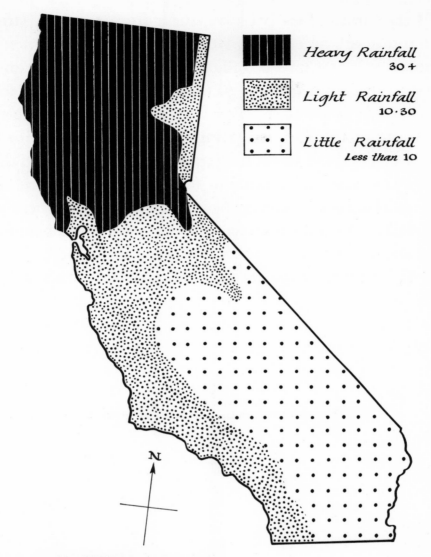

California water surpluses and deficiencies

It takes a rainfall of about 20 inches a year to farm without irrigation. Many places in the United States get that many inches. But most of the places on the West Coast do not get 20 inches. In some places, in the northern part, there are heavy rains during the winter. Much of the water runs away into rivers and the ocean. Some places are like deserts where there is little rain and almost never a cloud in the sky. Water has to be brought to this dry land.

79

Large areas of the West depend upon irrigation. Most of the irrigation water comes from melting snow of the high mountains. The Central Valley of California, between two ranges of mountains, is one of the richest valleys to be found anywhere. It is a warm valley with not nearly enough rainfall. Large amounts of irrigation water are needed. Some of this water comes from rivers, some from water behind dams. Many plans have been made to bring water to this and other California valleys. More crops could be grown if there were more water. As time goes on and there are more people living in the United States, there will have to be more food. So water for growing crops becomes more important all the time.

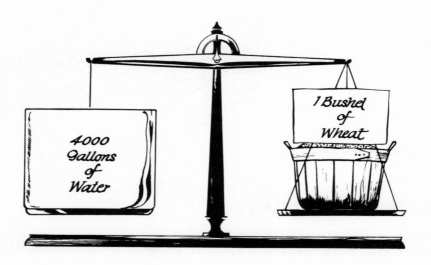

15. Water in the city

T HE WATER in your faucet had a very long journey. Can you trace this journey? If you can, you know that the water came from a huge pipe under the street. Since this pipe under the street is the main pipe, it is called the water main. In cities today there are thousands of these huge water mains.

Before water came to the water main, it probably traveled a hundred miles or more. The Romans had to use pipes to bring water to their cities. They called such pipes by the same name as we do, "aqueducts." "Aqua" means "water," and "duct" means "lead." So water is led through pipes to places where it is needed. We will tell later about some large cities that have had to build large aqueducts. Where does the water in your city come from?

Did you ever stop to think how water reaches to the top floor of a tall building? How did it get "uphill" so far? Pump stations driven by electric motors gave it the "push" up into high buildings.

Pumping station (U.S. Bureau of Reclamation)

In city homes water has many uses, old and new. It is used for drinking, cooking, heating. It is used to keep our bodies and clothes clean. Pipes carry waste water from the kitchen, the tub, the toilet. Water is used for lawns and gardens.

You can think of many ways in which a modern city uses water. Milk bottles must be washed before milk can be put into them. Think of the many foods and drinks you buy in bottles and cans for which water is used. Then there are swimming pools, water fountains, and car laundries. Factories in cities use a great deal of water. The city uses water to clean streets.

82

Water is used to put out fires. In the old days fire-fighting was quite different. When there was a call of FIRE! each man nearby grabbed a bucket. Two lines stood along the street between a pump and the burning house. The man nearest the pump filled buckets as fast as he could. He passed each bucket to the next man and so on down the line. The other line of men passed along the empty buckets to be filled again. Everyone helped his neighbor. Now we depend on huge fire trucks with great long fire hoses to put out fires. All this is part of living in a modern city.

Where do you think water goes after it has been used? Pipes carry waste from the sink in the kitchen, from the

The water in the city has come a long way (U.S. Bureau of Reclamation)

83

washbasin, and the toilet. The waste flows through pipes into a still-larger pipe in the street. This pipe is like the main water pipe except that it carries waste instead of fresh water. These large pipes are sewer pipes. You have seen gratings at street corners near curbs. These carry waste water from the street into the sewer below too. Sewer pipes carry waste water or sewage to sewage-treatment plants. These plants are usually near a river or the ocean. Here water is made clean enough to flow into the river or ocean. If it were not for this, there could be no swimming or other use of the water.

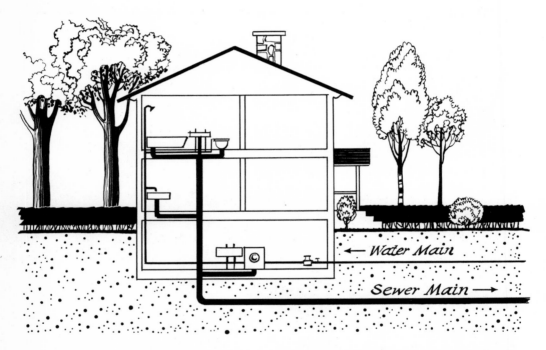

Cities are growing larger and larger. In the future there will be uses for water that we have never dreamed about. What do you suppose water will be used for next? And where will we get it? There must be plenty of water for the cities in the years ahead as well as now. People in days gone by had to plan how to get more water for their needs. We have to think and plan about it too.

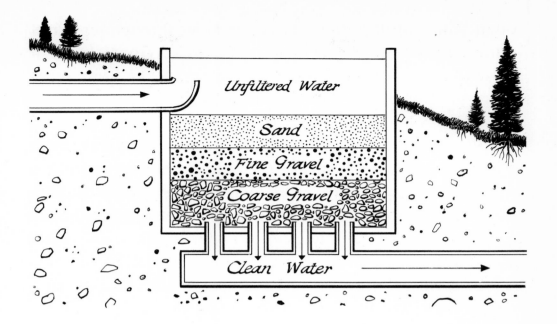

16. Clean water

WE MUST not just have water. It must be clean water, safe for drinking. When water is not clean, we say that it is polluted. Polluted water is not fit for use in homes.

One way that water is polluted is by having silt in it. Silt, you will remember, is the soil that makes rivers and streams brown and muddy. When a heavy rain carries the soil with it into some streams, both land and water are harmed. It would not cost so much to make water clean if more care were taken to keep soil from washing away in the first place.

Waste such as oils or acids from factories are sometimes found in streams. Waste from homes (sewage) is put into them. This water is not good for people to use. Fish cannot live in it, either. Something should be done to keep water clean.

When water is polluted in any way, engineers change it into safe water for drinking. One way this is done is to filter water. Water is run into a storage basin with sand and gravel in the bottom. The water is allowed to seep slowly through the sand. Then it is passed through the gravel and into pipes having screens. From there the clean water is sent to pumping stations and on to homes.

Water that is very brown and muddy has to have even more done to it. A chemical called alum is added to it. This makes something that looks like jelly. After a while the jelly sinks to the bottom. Down the dirt goes to the bottom! The alum soaks it up and only clean water is left.

Water must be not only clean but pure. Did you ever hear of germs? Germs are tiny plants and animals. You cannot see them, but they are powerful just the same. Some are good and some are bad. The water we drink must have no germs that hurt us. They are so small they cannot be filtered out. Something else has to be done. Chlorine is added to water. Have you ever been in a swimming pool that had chlorine in it? It is added to swimming water for the same reason. The small amount added to water does not hurt people but it kills germs. This is very important to people's health.

Sewage is the waste from kitchens, bathrooms, and laundries. This waste water can be made clean again. There are sewage plants that do this. Sewage water is put into large tanks and as it moves slowly inside the tanks, the heavy particles go to the bottom. This is called sludge. The lighter materials go to the top. Sludge is dried and sold as fertilizer. The rest of the water is filtered.

Sometimes all that is needed to make water pure is sun and air. Odor in the water is often taken out this way too.

Wild animals and fish need pure water. If it is not pure, they will either go to another place to live or die. So keeping water clean helps wild life as well as people.

17. How much water is enough?

TODAY America has nearly 186,000,000* people. At present it looks as if there will be over 3,000,000 more people each year, or about 225,000,000 by 1975.

Many cities are worried that there will not be enough water for people who live here. More people means that more water will be used. More people means that there will have to be more food grown. This will take lots more water. Factories will have to make more things, and that means that they too will need more water. It is feared that there will be too many people for the amount of water we have.

We have been sending food to many nations that do not have enough food for their people. In the future will we have enough water in the right places to grow enough for our own food supply? This is the question that is being asked. It is enough to make all of us think. We cannot feed more and more with less and less. And we cannot just think of what is needed NOW. We have to think about what will happen ten years from now, and on and on.

* U.S. Census Bureau figure, as of July 1, 1962.

There was not enough water here (U.S. Bureau of Reclamation)

At present, when you turn on your faucet, water is there. If you want a bath, there is plenty of water to keep you clean. If you want to water your garden and lawn, water gushes out. We cannot be sure that this will always be so. The time may come when no water or very little will come from the faucet. The reservoirs from which our water is piped could become empty.

Suppose you saw in the paper:

Faucets may be used between 7:00 in the morning and 1:00 in the afternoon each day.

This will be enough for family use.

Drink and use as little as you can.

No water is to be used to water flowers or lawns.

All those who do not obey will be fined $100 or be put in jail.

This sounds too strange to be true, doesn't it? But it has happened in some parts of our country already.

One way of having more water is to save more of the rainfall. Another is to keep hillsides and watersheds green so that rain will soak in and not run off. And water must be brought from places where there is too much water to places where it is needed most.

Even now we are short of water. There is hardly a day that goes by that some newspaper does not tell about this, especially in the West. Look at this map. It is easy to see

YEARLY RAINFALL

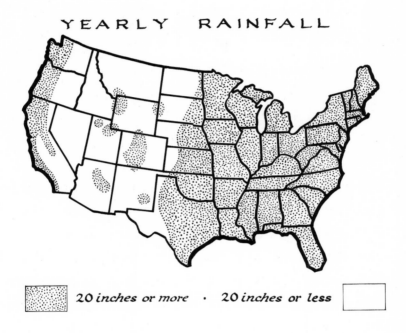

☐ *20 inches or more* · *20 inches or less* ☐

which part of the United States has the least water and which has the most rainfall. And yet we know that most of the food is grown where there is the least water.

We also know that it takes a long time to plan and build dams and aqueducts. Usually this takes years. That means that plans have to be made a long time before there is a very serious need. Where there is a shortage of water there is no time to lose.

We have learned that conservation is "saving together" for the NOW and the FUTURE. And that is what we have to do!

18. *The search for water*

H OW CAN we have enough water for the needs of all the people? Only man can plan what to do. He cannot "grow" water as he does plants and trees! But he can think of ways to save and use the water we have. We should be glad that there are trained people who are searching for water all the time. But we can all help in some way. First we must know how important water is to all of us.

We know that engineers have gone hundreds of miles away from cities in search of more water for city use. We know that they have planned irrigation canals that bring water to farmlands. This planning goes on all the time. Aqueducts and dams have been built that cost a great deal of money. There are those who try to think of other ways of getting water by spending less money.

Some people think that we could use water from the ocean. There is plenty of water there! Cities cannot use the ocean water for drinking because it is too salty. Farmers cannot use such water for crops because salty water would kill plants. But ways have been found to take salt out of water. If you boil salty water, the salt does not change to steam. The salt stays in the pan; only the water is changed to steam. If the steam vapor is cooled, it is changed back to water. Now it is water without salt. Water made in this way is called distilled water. This is the kind of water that is put in batteries of automobiles. It is also the kind that comes in bottles and is used by people for drinking. Then why not distill ocean water so that people can use it? We may have to do this, but at present distilled water made from ocean water costs too much. Then, too, it would have to be pumped to places where

Planned irrigation that brings water to farmlands (California Water Resources Bureau)

it was needed. A cheaper way to distill ocean water may be found in the near future.

Another way of getting water to places where it is needed is by "seeding the clouds." This is a way of making clouds "rain" when they would not otherwise do so. The "rain maker" takes an airplane high into the clouds. Then he sprays tiny ice crystals into them. The tiny droplets in the clouds gather around the crystals. Tiny drops become big drops. Down the rain falls! Another way is to set up a machine that sprays silver iodide into the air to seed the clouds. It is man's way of making nature work for him. The trouble is that there are not always clouds about! Also there are those who think it is not right to do this. Not all people want rain at the same time in an area. Too much rain could fall and cause floods.

We shall have to learn more about making clean water out of unclean water, too. There are billions and billions of gallons of water that go down the drains from homes and factories. This waste water could be used again. Some cities (such as Los Angeles) have a way of taking sewer water and making it clean and pure again. Cities and factories are working to see how this can best be done. So far this way of making pure water from unclean water costs too much. The time may come when some method will have to be used if there is to be enough water where it is most needed.

19. Water for thirsty lands

MOST OF the people in the United States live where rain falls during the growing season. Year in and year out the farmer in the East and Midwest expects rain to water his crops. In the Southwestern part of the United States there is very little rain. Washington, D.C., has four times as much rain as Arizona. Twenty million acres of land in the seventeen Western states have to use irrigation for their crops.

In California little rain falls in the summer. This is the time when water is needed most. There is a lot of sunshine, but nature is selfish with its water. Cities in Southern California know that they must have more water for all the people who are coming there. Farmers know that, unless water is brought to their land, there will be few crops. Californians have had to plan how to get water and use it wisely. It has been so from the beginning.

When the mission fathers (*padres*) came to California, they looked for places to build their missions. They built

93

them where Indians lived, usually in a fertile valley and always where there was some water. These mission fathers were the first ones in the state to build dams and canals. Behind the mission in Santa Barbara they built a dam in a canyon. Two large stone basins were built on the hillside below it. One canal went through the gardens to Santa Barbara. The other ran through the mission grounds to a fountain. Even when there was little rainfall, Santa Barbara seemed to have enough water. The interesting early-day reservoir can still be seen near the mission. Parts of the stone aqueduct can be traced from the canyon to the mission fountain. One of the basins was made so well it is still used by the city of Santa Barbara.

The mission fathers were California's first farmers. At the mission in Ventura (Mission San Buenaventura) the padres worked hard to plant vegetables and grains. The soil was good but there was not enough water. The padres taught the Indians how to dam up water to catch and hold the rainfall. They built canals from the dam. Ventura was sometimes called "the place of canals." One of the canals was seven miles long. Vegetables grew there better than in any other place in the state.

Water was very important to the miners who came to find gold in California. At first the miners "panned" for gold in the streams. This way seemed much too slow for them. They kept trying to find faster and easier ways to get gold. Finally they tried HYDRAULIC MINING. Water was brought in long ditches or wooden troughs. Then it was sent through pipes to a large hose. The hose sprayed against the hillsides. The force caused the earth that had gold ore in it to break apart. Whole hills were washed down. Thousands of tons of soil and rocks were washed into canyons and streams. After a while hydraulic mining filled up rivers with mud.

94

Water was very important to the miners who came to find gold in California (California Bureau of Mines, San Francisco)

There were floods after heavy rains. Farmlands were ruined. Hydraulic mining had to be stopped.

Miners returned from the gold fields. Many had not found the gold they wanted. They looked for land. Most of the *ranchos* (farms) were in Southern California. No one seemed to be living on the many acres of rich land. So they decided to stay and become farmers. Each man had to take care of his own water problem.

Dry years came when no rain fell. This was in 1864 and 1865. Cattle by the thousands died all over the state. Green fields turned to brown. People left ranchos and went to live in the pueblos. Pueblos grew into towns. Towns grew into cities.

As long as Los Angeles was a small city, there was enough water close by. As the city grew, more water was needed. About 1908, Los Angeles knew that it would have to go farther away to get water. A place was found on the eastern side of the Sierra Nevada mountains. But this was two hundred miles away! The aqueduct from the Owens River there would have to cross a desert (Mojave) and go through mountains. No matter—Los Angeles had to have water. Dams were built to make reservoirs and for electric

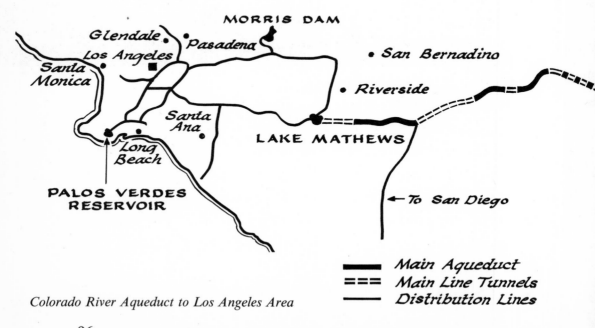

Colorado River Aqueduct to Los Angeles Area

power. It took five years to build the dams, tunnels, and pipe lines that brought water to the growing city.

But even this was not enough! More and more people came to Los Angeles to live. More and more crops had to be grown. More and more factories . . . more and more everything! More water again had to be found—and soon!

Far away on the border of Arizona and Nevada was the long, winding Colorado River. For many years the river had flowed over its banks and flooded farms and towns. It was

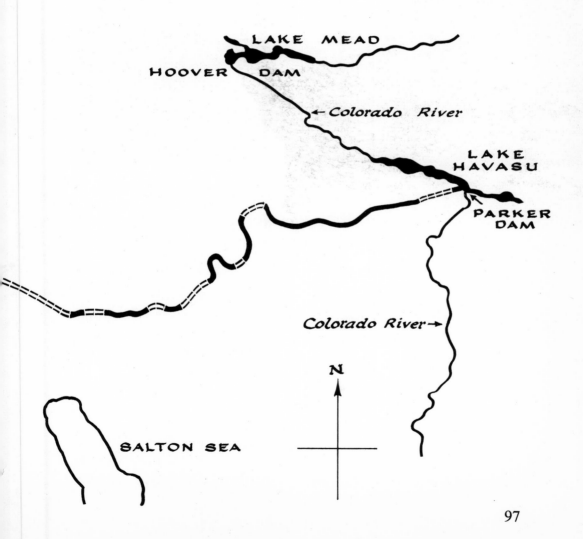

Hoover Dam by floodlight from Nevada side of Black Canyon (Hubert A. Lowman)

decided that water from this river should be used. A great dam, Hoover Dam, the highest in the United States, was built across the river. A canal was built and water brought from the dam to the rich but dry Imperial Valley. Water changed the valley from desert to a land of gardens! Seven states and Mexico agreed to build more canals and share the Colorado River water. An aqueduct brought water to Los Angeles, 340 miles away.

The story of water supply in San Francisco goes back to the days when it was the sleepy little village of Yerba Buena. At that time some of the people were able to get their water from nearby springs. Others had to buy water secured across the bay (in Sausalito), brought to their homes in barrels by water merchants. The price depended upon how far up a hill the people lived!

Then gold was discovered in California (1848) near Sacramento. The closest harbor was San Francisco (the new name given to Yerba Buena). It suddenly became the center of the gold rush. Thousands of people came from all over the world to seek gold. San Francisco became a city almost overnight. One of the first needs was more water. Water from a creek nearby (Lobos Creek) was used. Water was pumped up to two reservoirs on top of Russian Hill. Pipes from the two reservoirs (still in use) brought water to the people of the new San Francisco.

It was not long (between 1867–90) before planners saw that still more water was needed. Engineers knew that water would have to come from farther away. They went to San Mateo County, where three dams (two of earth, one of cement, can still be seen today) were built across streams. Water from reservoirs behind dams came through pipes to the city. Now it seemed that San Francisco would have plenty of water for a long time!

As San Francisco grew, so grew the need for more water. There were those who knew that a city could not grow any faster than its water supply. These planners and engineers looked ahead to future needs. In 1920 Calaveras Dam (between Alameda and Santa Clara counties) was built. At that time it was the highest earth-fill dam in the world. Melting snows from nearby Mount Hamilton filled the reservoir behind the huge dam. Pipes under the bay brought water to San Francisco.

Still this supply of water was not enough. Private companies had built the dams and supplied the water before.

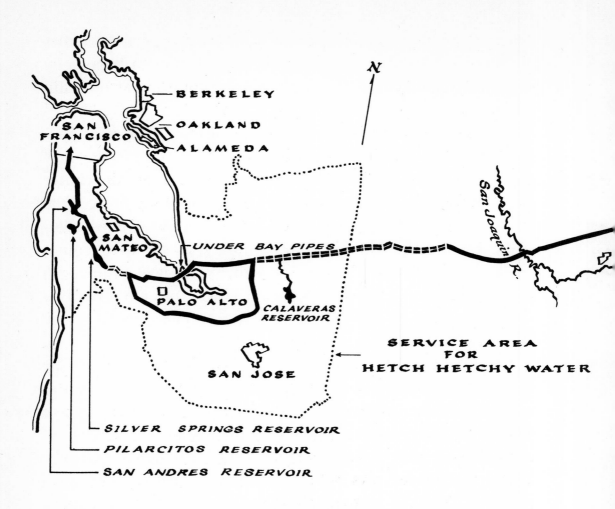

Hetch Hetchy water is brought to the San Francisco area

Now the city of San Francisco itself took a hand. The federal government gave permission to the city to get water from the mountains in Yosemite National Park. Many years were spent in planning before any actual work was done on the new water system.

Finally dams were built to hold back mountain streams, rainfall runoff, and melting snow. The largest one was O'Shaughnessy Dam. Pipe lines were laid across valleys and through mountains. In 1934, after twenty years of hard work, pure mountain water from the Hetch Hetchy area was brought

100

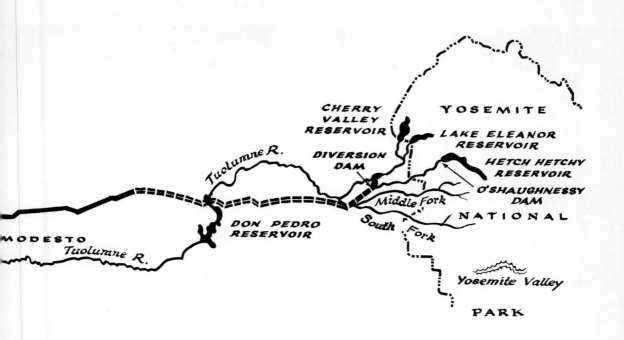

■ MAIN AQUEDUCT
== MAIN LINE TUNNELS

167 miles to San Francisco. Since then other pipe lines have brought water around the south end of the bay to cities there. Many industries have located there because of the good water supply.

San Francisco knows that even more water will be needed in years ahead and is already making plans for that time.

It is well known that the climate of California is "unusual." It is not even the same at both ends of the state. In the north where there are mountains there is lots of snow and rain. Two thirds of California's rainfall are in the north. In the Central Valley the summer is long with no rain. There

Hetch Hetchy Dam—Yosemite National Park (Hubert A. Lowman)

is a short season of winter rain. From San Francisco to San Diego along the coast there are ocean breezes and some fog. In certain parts of California (southeast) there is desert land. Here it is very hot in summer, with very little rain in winter.

If you should take an airplane trip over California (or look at a map), you would see that it is a long narrow state. You would see long mountain ranges. California is fortunate to have these mountains. The heavy winter snow slowly melts and the water from it fills streams. This water lasts well into the dry season. In between the mountains are valleys covered with farms and orchards that make California famous.

The Central Valley covers one third of the area of California. There are about six million acres here that need to be irrigated. The soil is rich and there is plenty of sunshine. The one thing that has always been needed is more water, especially in summer when it is hot and there is no rain. Over the years, as more people came and more crops were grown in the Central Valley, the need for water became even greater. Something had to be done to meet the problem. Since there was plenty of water in the Sacramento Valley to the north and not enough water in the San Joaquin Valley to the south, a plan was made to bring the water from the north to the south. This is why the Central Valley Project (started in 1935) came into being. Dams, canals, power plants, pools, and pumping plants had to be provided to bring water to the areas of the San Joaquin Valley where it was so much needed.

Shasta Dam was built high up in the Cascade Range (north of Redding) where melting snows and the runoff from heavy rainfall fed into the large Sacramento River. Water held back by the dam made Shasta Lake. Today, water from the lake is released through Shasta Dam and power plant. Some of the water is used to irrigate lands along the Sacramento River and in the delta area (see map on page 121). The Delta Cross Channel brings water through the delta area to a place near Tracy from which it is pumped up to the Delta-Mendota Canal. Through this canal the water flows toward the south to the Mendota Pool in the San Joaquin River (forty miles west of Fresno).

Friant Dam (see map on page 104) is another important part of the Central Valley Project. This dam was built across

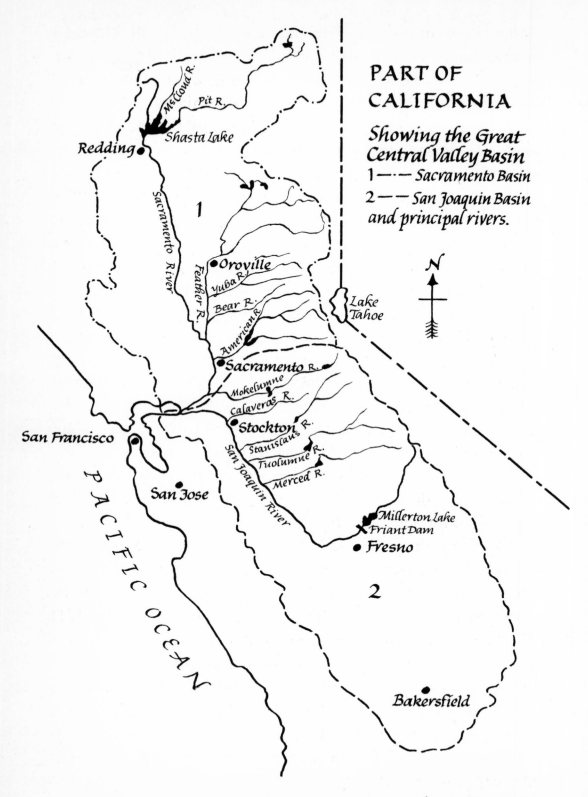

PART OF
CALIFORNIA

Showing the Great
Central Valley Basin
1 —·— Sacramento Basin
2 — — San Joaquin Basin
and principal rivers.

N

McCloud R.

Pit R.

Shasta Lake

Redding

Sacramento River

1

Feather R.

Oroville

Yuba R.

Bear R.

American R.

Lake Tahoe

Sacramento R.

Mokelumne

Calaveras R.

San Francisco

Stockton R.

Stanislaus

Tuolumne R.

San Jose

Merced R.

San Joaquin River

PACIFIC OCEAN

Millerton Lake
Friant Dam

Fresno

2

Bakersfield

104

the San Joaquin River not far from the valley. Behind the dam water is stored in Millerton Lake (twenty-one miles northeast of Fresno). Below the dam water flows through the Friant-Kern Canal for over 150 miles to a point near Bakersfield. This canal supplies water for irrigation to the east side of the San Joaquin Valley in Fresno, Tulare, and Kern counties (see

Shasta Dam, lake and powerhouse (U.S. Bureau of Reclamation)

map on page 121). Water from Friant Dam also flows into the Madera Canal for parts of Madera County to the north.

The water from the Sacramento River that is put into the San Joaquin River at Mendota Pool replaces the water that is diverted from the San Joaquin River at Friant Dam.

The San Joaquin Valley produces many millions of dollars' worth of crops and livestock. More kinds of crops and in greater amounts are produced here than in any other part of the state. It is easy to see why water is so important to this area and to all of California. Industries and cities gain also by having the resources of both power and water.

Over and above the irrigated crops, water for the needs of people, and energy from powerplants, the Central Valley Project is important to the state's recreation areas and the fisheries. Water areas provide places for many kinds of waterfowl. All of these things are part of the "conservation story" —making wise use of our resources for the most people for the longest time.

The Feather River Project (which is a part of an all-over California Water Plan) is one that will share the water of the north with the southern part of the state (see map of the Feather River Project). The plan is to take water from areas that have more than enough water and bring it to parts of California that need more water. Some two thirds of the land where water is needed is in the south and central part of the state. More than half of the people in California live in the southern part of California.

About 70 per cent of California's water is in the north. At times some areas have floods and water runs away to be wasted. Southern California has only 2 per cent of the state's water resources and receives less than one-fifth as much rainfall as northern California.

Because the Feather River Project is a plan that would

106

FEATHER RIVER
PROJECT
CALIFORNIA

N

OREGON

NEVADA

NEVADA

Oroville Reservoir
and Dam
• Oroville

Feather R.

Sacramento
River→ • Sacramento

Lake Tahoe

Delta Pool
• Stockton

San Francisco
• Oakland

San Luis Reservoir
and Dam

• Fresno

San Joaquin Valley –
Southern California Aqueduct Route

Reservoir

San Luis Obispo

• Bakersfield

Santa Barbara

• Los
Angeles

• San Bernardino

Long Beach

Perris Reservoir

Colorado River

ARIZONA

• San Diego

MEXICO

107

provide flood control in certain areas and more water where it is badly needed, the project is an important one. Such a project would have a system of canals, reservoirs, tunnels, and pumping plants. It would take water from northern California to areas in the south.

Even though there is a great need for more water for farming, factories, and people in the central and southern areas, the north wants to make sure that no plan is made that will take too much water away from the north. It takes a long time to study such matters, to agree, to plan, and to build. Great sums of money have to be spent. These are reasons why plans have to be made far ahead of the time of need.

The resources, beauty, and pleasant climate of California make it an important state. It seems to have everything but one—water in all parts of the state. And what happens to California's farmlands is important to all the states in the nation. By irrigating California's fertile valleys America can have more food for its people. California leads all the states in value of crops grown. Half of the fruits and vegetables in the United States come from the rich valleys. California sends the fruits of its orchards to the tables of the world! From California come 80 to 100 per cent of all figs, avocados, grapes, prunes, olives, lemons, almonds, dates, and many other fruits.

California is growing more than any other state in the United States, at the rate of sixteen hundred people a day! In 1910 there were about two and a half million people living in California. In 1962, over seventeen million. California is second to New York in the number of people living there. Some say that there will be twenty million people before too long and that it will have more people than any other state. As more people come, more houses have to be built. This

108

means that there are fewer and fewer acres of farmlands. It also means that there will be more and more factories and more need for water.

Where will California's growth lead? The future depends on water. So it is thought that WATER is the key to the West. Never has there been such interest as today in California's water. Other states, too, may run short of water. There may be years of little rainfall, dry wells, or reservoirs. The water table is falling in many places. This state is an example of what can be done in water conservation. It is planning for present and future needs. The eyes of America are on California!

Look at the sky and the clouds (Karl Obert, A.P.S.A.)

20. We can all help

DO YOU think that conservation plans are so huge that you can do little about them? You may say, "Why should I know about these things? That's for the farmer—and I'm not going to be a farmer." That may be true. But by this time you know that we all get our living from the soil in one way or another. Poor land makes poor people no matter where they live. The farmer may not have enough for his own family's needs. Then what of people in the cities? We all have to have food and water to live. No one is too young to understand that. So wherever you live—in the North, South, East, or West— we are partners together. The more we learn about our land and its resources, the easier it will be to use them wisely.

From now on you will be interested and thinking about all these things. You will meet people who think that the care of resources such as soil is not important. You know that they are most important. You can tell them why. It is one thing to know and understand. It is something else to do something about it!

110

All of us can begin with what is around us. You don't have to go any farther away than your home or school ground. Look at a slope or a low place in your own yard. Have you planted seeds to see what will grow there? You will see how important soil is as a home for plants. If you don't water the plants, you will see how important water is to them. There is something exciting about asking why and then finding out the answer for yourself.

Make a trip to a field or vacant lot or into the country, especially after a rainstorm. See how soil has been washed from slopes? Do you see that the fine soil has been washed down? See that soil did not wash off where it was covered with grass or shrubs? Erosion is something that will have to be fought all the time.

You do not have to go to a national park to see nature at work. In your yard or the park you can see nature living and working with itself. When you see a bird or a bee hovering over a flower, roses in the garden, a crow in the field, a beaver in a stream, find out which is giving, which is taking. Think what your place in nature is, too. How do YOU fit into nature's pattern?

Be interested in weather. See how it affects the land where you live. Look at the sky and the clouds. See what rain does. The radio, newspaper, and TV tell about weather every day.

If you live where water is scarce, you will want to know how it can be saved and used more wisely. If you live where there is lots of water, you may find out what is done about floods. If your home is on a farm, you can learn about the best ways of using soil and water. You can help plant trees and grass to hold water in the soil. Our government spends lots of time and money studying and working out plans for us. The least we can do is try to understand and help if we can.

Everyone can help in a few simple ways. We should be

Range land being seeded and fertilized so that grass may grow again (George Borst)

careful not to leave water running when not in use. Dripping faucets and leaky pipes are water wasters. If you raise plants, you should learn the best ways to water them. Perhaps you should use less water and water them in the cooler part of the day. Do not throw trash into streams. Be careful about fires, especially in wooded places.

If you are careful to do these simple things you will be helping to guard the beauty and usefulness of your state.

112

Planting seedling pine trees after a fire (California Division of Forestry)

Did you ever hear of young people who helped by planting trees? The Los Angeles schools, for example, have camp centers where this is done. One of them is Clear Creek Camp. In ten years young people have planted 75,000 pine trees on 250 acres. It was lots of fun, too.

Every year in the spring (March) there is Conservation Week. Take part and see what you can do to understand and help.

You will not always be as young as you are now, of course. As you grow older you may be able to help in many ways. You

Men go high into the mountains to measure snowfall (Soil Conservation Service—U.S.D.A.)

114

may belong to a group that studies about conservation. As time goes on and there are more needs, more and more studies will have to be made. Perhaps someday you may join men who go high into the mountains to measure the snowfall or rainfall. Maybe you will be one who works to prevent floods and wasted water. You could be one who helps farmers in conservation districts by testing soils or making maps for better use of land. There is plenty of interesting work for a conservationist.

Maybe you will be an engineer who plans or builds dams or aqueducts. You may work as a forest ranger or as a weatherman. It may be that you will be one who teaches others. You could be one who makes laws about the conservation of soil and water. You may have to vote for such laws. No doubt you will have to pay taxes and will want to know how the tax money is spent. Whether you live on a farm or in a city, you will always be interested and want to care for the resources we have.

America has always been a rich and beautiful place. If we work as PARTNERS—every man, woman, and child—we can keep it that way. We may even pass on an even richer country to those who come after us. Everyone should want to have a part in doing this. We live in a country where everyone wants to do his share. What are we going to do with our country's resources? Will there be PLENTY or WASTE? Of course we all want plenty. Then we must not waste. Will we have RICHES or RUIN? What are YOU going to do to help?

Let's keep America green (California Division of Forestry)

116

Words to know

CANAL	a ditch for water
CANYON	a deep valley with steep sides
CONDENSE	water vapor turns into drops of water
CONSERVATION	wise use of resources
CONTOUR PLANTING	planting which follows the curve of the land
EROSION	the eating away or wearing away of the land
EVAPORATE	to pass off as a gas
FERTILE LAND	land in which plants grow well
GULLY	a deep cut in the soil caused by running water
HUMUS	a mixture of rotted leaves, twigs, weeds
HYDRAULIC MINING	mining by spraying water against hillsides
HYDROELECTRIC POWER	electricity made by water power
IRRIGATION	watering crops by means of canals and ditches
MINERAL	that which is neither animal or vegetable
PADRE	mission father
PLANT COVER	the covering of plants which protect the soil
POLLUTION OF WATER	that which makes water unclean
PUEBLO	village
RANCHO	farm
RESERVOIR	storage basin
RESOURCE, NATURAL	nature's gifts to us, such as soil, water, minerals
ROTATION PLANTING	planting of different kinds of crops during succeeding years
SEWAGE	waste from bathrooms, etc., carried by sewers
SOIL	land in which plants grow
WATER VAPOR	water evaporated into the air, a gas
WATERSHED	slopes that hold rain water and snow—nature's storage place or reservoir
WATER TABLE	the top level of water stored under the ground

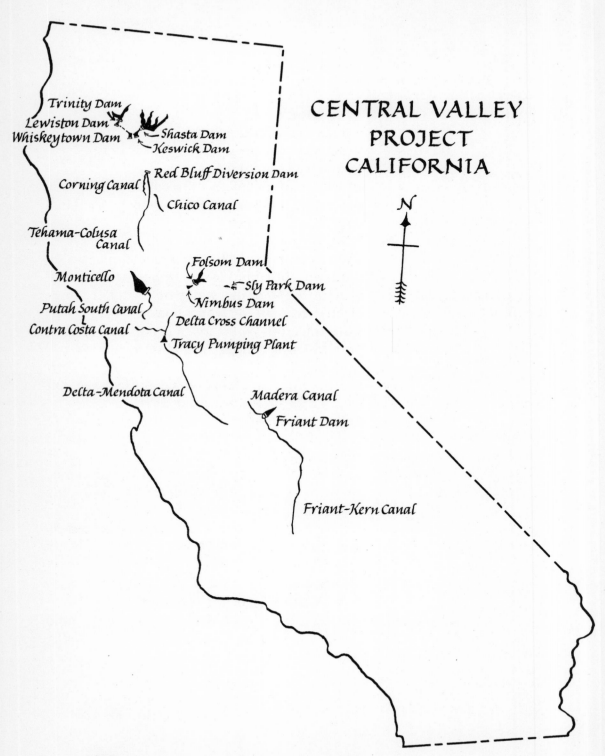

Trinity Dam
Lewiston Dam
Whiskeytown Dam
Shasta Dam
Keswick Dam
Red Bluff Diversion Dam
Corning Canal
Chico Canal
Tehama-Colusa Canal
Folsom Dam
Monticello
Sly Park Dam
Nimbus Dam
Putah South Canal
Delta Cross Channel
Contra Costa Canal
Tracy Pumping Plant
Delta-Mendota Canal
Madera Canal
Friant Dam
Friant-Kern Canal

CENTRAL VALLEY
PROJECT
CALIFORNIA

N

Index

119

120